Drying Herbs

An essential guide on drying herbs for Kitchen Spices and Seasonings

By Elisa Howard

Copyright 2016 - All Rights Reserved – Elisa Howard

ALL RIGHTS RESERVED. No part of this publication may be reproduced or transmitted in any form whatsoever, electronic, or mechanical, including photocopying, recording, or by any informational storage or retrieval system without express written, dated and signed permission from the author.

Table of Contents

INTRODUCTION — 4

CHAPTER 1 — 5
What are Herbs? — 5

CHAPTER 2 — 10
How to Prepare to Dry Herbs — 10

CHAPTER 3 — 16
Tips on Harvesting Different Parts of Herbal Plants — 16

CHAPTER 4 — 21
Methods Used for Drying Herbs — 21

CHAPTER 5 — 28
How You Can Dry and Store Your Herbs — 28

CHAPTER 6 — 34
List of Herbs: Kitchen Spices and Seasonings — 34

CONCLUSION — 41

INTRODUCTION

You may buy dried herbs from the supermarket or herb store, but, most of these herbs may have been there for a long time. Herbs take long to get spoilt, but they lose their color and flavor as they age. Growing and drying your own herbs is an easier way of getting fresh and organic herbs when you need them. They can be right there on your kitchen shelf, cupboard or drawer making you a proud herb user who has colorful, flavorings with all the fresh aromas that make food so appealing.

You may grow herbs in pots, containers or in your herb garden and harvest them regularly. Preserving them is even better because you will just reach out to them even when they are out of season. You can preserve them when they produce faster than you use them. They may grow so quickly that, you cannot keep up with them at the rate you harvest and use them. Fortunately, you have the option of drying them since you wouldn't want to watch them get wasted. This book will show you how you can dry them and then store them for a long time to come.

Chapter 1

What are Herbs?

Herbs can be dried and preserved for use as kitchen spices and seasonings. Many people enjoy food flavored with spices and seasonings but herbs can be used for other purposes as well. Drying your own herbs ensures that you have colorful and fresh-tasting herbs that are grown organically. They have more color, flavor and preserved essential oils than those bought in supermarkets and stores.

What are herbs and spices?

Some people really wonder whether there is a difference between herbs and spices. Herbs are obtained from the leafy green parts of these plants, and they can either be fresh or dried. Herbs are the leaves of herbaceous plants. Herbaceous plants are non- woody plants. Examples of herbs include Basil, Bay Leaf, Cilantro, Mint, and Parsley. Herbs are commonly used as food, flavorings, perfumes, and for medicinal purposes. They are also used as vegetables and for garnishing, stuffing and pickling among other uses.

Spices refer to the products from any other part of the plant such as seeds, roots, bark, berries, fruits and flowers or buds. They are usually dried before use and are generally aromatic. Examples of spices include Cinnamon, Chives, Garlic, Ginger, Nutmeg, and Cloves. Spices are generally used as flavorings, preservatives and colorings. Many spices are rich in antimicrobial properties and are used in meats, fish, poultry and other foods that are prone to getting spoilt. This may also explain why they are used in warmer climates where infectious diseases are common. Spices can be used as an ingredient in the production of perfumes, cosmetics and for medicinal purposes and as vegetables.

In some cases both herbs and spices can be obtained from the same plant such as Dill. The seeds from the Dill plant are spices, while the stalk of the plant is herbal.

Seasonings are herbs and spices both of which are referred individually as seasonings. When you add herbs, spices or salt to flavor your food, this process is known as seasoning.

Different Types of Spices

- Seeds and dried fruits include Black pepper, Cumin, Mustard, Fennel and Nutmeg.
- Barks include Cinnamon and Cassia.
- Flower buds include dried Cloves.
- Stigmas such as Saffron from saffron crocus.
- Roots and rhizomes include Garlic, Ginger, and Turmeric.
- Resins such as Asafoetida.

Herbs may be used as spices and seasonings to flavor food, but it is good to note that, spices are usually stronger in flavor and fragrance than other herbs because they are concentrated. They should therefore be used in moderation unless the user likes hot foods with plenty of spices. Use smaller quantities when flavoring.

Choosing Herbs for Drying

There are many herbs, which you can harvest and dry for use as kitchen spices and seasonings. They are so many varieties on this planet some of which are grown at home and others harvested in the wild, than we could possibly list. Most of them, which qualify for drying, are commonly grown in many home gardens and pots.

There are some herbs, which retain most of their flavor when they are frozen although they can be dried. These include Basil, Chives,

Cilantro, Lemongrass, Mint and Parsley among others. To freeze them, chop them after cleaning and them place them in ice cube trays. Cover them with water and then put them in the freezer or mix them with some olive oil instead of water before freezing. Use these frozen herbs mostly in soups, stews, sauces or stir-fries.

Other herbs, which you can harvest for drying, include:

Leaves

Bay, Basil, Celery, Chervil, Dill, Geranium, Lemon balm, Lemon verbena, Lovage, Marjoram, Oregano, Rosemary, Sage, Summer savory, Tarragon, and Thyme.

Seeds

Anise, Caraway, Celery, Chervil, Cloves, Coriander, Cumin, Dill, Fennel, and Mustard.

Flowers

Bee balm, Chamomile, Chive, Dill, Geranium, Lavender, Linden, Marigold, Nasturtium, Rose, Thyme, and Yarrow.

Fruits

Hot peppers.

Roots

Garlic, Ginger, Horseradish etc. Roots take longer to dry than leaves and seeds.

Using Dried Spices and Seasonings

Herbs have been used for centuries in many parts of the world. Most herbs are indigenous and they have been used for thousands of years when cooking different types of foods, as flavorings. They are also used as preservatives, for medicinal purposes and as perfumes, cosmetics and disinfectants. That is why preserving them by drying is so important. Today, we still use herbs for different purposes mainly as spices and seasonings for flavoring food. Many recipes include one or more herb ingredients whether fresh or in dried form. They ask you to add herbs as an ingredient when preparing or cooking foods and at times your favorite recipe may call for dried spices and seasonings. Even when the ingredients require fresh herbs, you can still substitute them with dried herbs but you have to use less amounts because they are concentrated. You can buy dried spices and seasonings from the supermarket or store but you can dry them yourself. It is easy, convenient and you save money that you can use on other things. If you want to dry them fast, use the microwave.

Dried herbs, which are stored whole can, stay for many years if they are stored well. Crushed herbs can be used for a year or longer and although they may not get spoilt, you should discard them when they lose their flavor. Keep harvesting and drying your herbs from time to time so you can have fresh dried herbs all the time. You will enjoy your foods more when they are flavored. Dried spices and seasonings are more concentrated than when they are harvested as fresh herbs. You should therefore use about 1 teaspoon crumbled dried leaves in place of a Tablespoon of fresh leaves. Spices are even more concentrated and you should use them in moderation unless you like very hot foods.

Although using whole herbs is better, you can prepare some blends, mixes and rubs in advance. You may keep some premixed ground blends to use for Italian recipes, Mexican dishes and barbecues. This can save you a lot of time when you are cooking these dishes. To make an Italian herb blend, mix 2-1/2 Tablespoons of each type of dried herbs such as Basil, Oregano and 1 full Tablespoon of dried Marjoram. Use a mortar and pestle to grind the ingredients. Store them in jars or containers and keep them in a cool dry place away from direct light. You can also use zipped plastic bags.

When substituting dried spices and seasoning in your recipes for fresh herbs, you should keep in mind that, the flavors and essential oils in the dried herbs are more concentrated than in fresh ones. That means that, you should use about half (1/2) of crumbled dried herbs, and about quarter (¼) of finely ground herbs for the same amount of fresh herbs you are substituting. Tea blends i.e. Peppermint and Fennel, are very popular. To use dried herbs in your teas, put about 1 teaspoon or 1 Tablespoon of the herbs (depending on the taste you want) and pour boiling water over the herbs. Steep the mixture for 5-10 minutes and then strain. You can take plain herbal tea or sweeten it. Use your favorite tea herbs and enjoy.

Chapter 2

How to Prepare to Dry Herbs

Drying herbs is a process that requires preparation just like anything else you do. You wouldn't want to harvest excess herbs that you can't use, unless you are ready to dry them. That doesn't mean that you keep procrastinating about drying your favorite herbs. The methods are simple and they work fast, and you can dry your herbs any time you want.

Choose the method you want to use

There are many methods you can use to dry your herbs. Some like air-drying are easy and inexpensive. However, air-drying is not appropriate in some weathers and climates. Drying in the microwave retains the color and flavor of the herbs while dehydrator drying requires you to buy the machine or make a simple one with cardboards or plywood. Microwave drying works best for those herbs that have low moisture, such as Parsley, Rosemary, Marjoram, Oregano, and Dill. Herbs that contain a lot of moisture such as Basil, Mint and Chives are best dried either in a dehydrator or in the oven.

Harvest the herbs

You can harvest your herbs at any time but the best time is in mid-morning when the dew has dried from the leaves. It is most ideal to harvest your herbs before flowering unless you want to harvest flowers. If you've been harvesting the herbs regularly, your plants may not have had a chance of flowering, so you can harvest and dry them at any time. Usually, non-hardy herbs start declining as the weather cools, so it is better to harvest and dry them in late summer.

To retain most of flavor, cut herbs in mid-morning, right after the morning dew has dried but don't wait until the heat of the sun has dried the essential oils. You need these healthy essential oils so time your harvesting well. It's also good to pick the plants before they start wilting because of the afternoon sun.

To harvest, cut the healthy branches and stems from the herbal plants which you plan to dry. Remove all the spotted, diseased, dry and wilted leaves. Any leaves that have a yellow color and those leaves, which have spots, may be diseased so you wouldn't want to dry them. The flavor of such herbs will have diminished.

Remove all the lower leaves, which are about 1 inch from the branch.

Hold the stems or branches with your hands and shake them gently so that any insects holding onto them will fall or fly away. Get rid of any dirt before you start drying.

If you picked your herbs by uprooting the plants, you should shake off the soil.

Some plants need to be cleaned and so you should rinse them in cool water and pat dry them with air towels gently. Rinse the herbs by running cool water over them in a colander. You can use a salad spinner to dry the herbs if you have one. Don't dry all at the same time, dry a few at a time. If you don't have a salad spinner, pat the herbs between layers of paper towels to remove as much water as possible especially if you are using a microwave or oven to dry them otherwise they will get cooked because of the moisture instead of drying.

Herb leaves should be harvested when the essential oils in the plants are highest. Leafy herbs such as Basil, Chervil, Marjoram, and Savory can be harvested before they blossom. Other herbs like Basil, Coriander, Cilantro, Lemon balm, Mint Parsley, Rosemary, and Sage can be cut many times during the growing season.

Bunch drying

This is an easy way to dry many herbs, which have long stems such as Basil, Sage, Mint, Parsley, Dill, Marjoram, Rosemary and Savory among many others.

If the leaves are clean, you may dry them without washing to avoid losing oils during rinsing. However, if the herbs are dirty or dusty, you should rinse them gently under cool water. Shake the herbs to remove excess water and tie them in small bunches for hanging.

- Hold 4 - 6 branches or 5-10 stems together depending on their size and tie them as a bunch. You can use a string, strong thread or a rubber band. The rubber band is better because the bundles will keep shrinking as they dry and the rubber band will adjust. However, keep checking from time to time that the herbs are not falling off and tighten the rubber band. Tie smaller bundles if you are drying herbs with high moisture levels.
- Hang the herbs somewhere so the water can evaporate.
- Take the herb bunches indoors and hang them upside down with the stems facing up and the leafy ends down. Hang them in a warm, dry place where there is enough air circulation. Choose a well-ventilated place which does not receive direct sunlight.
- Hanging herbs upside down ensures that the essential oils in the stems flow into the leaves. Don't hang them near any heated area like above a stove because odors and heat may damage the flavor, texture, and aroma.
- To prevent dust from collecting on the drying leaves, place each bunch inside a paper bag before hanging. Gather the top of the bag and tie it loosely so the leaves can hang freely. For ventilation, punch holes in the bag.
- Label each paper bag with the name of the herb and the date.
- Hang the herb bundles upside down so the leaves face downwards inside the bags. Ensure that the herbs are not congested inside the bag so they can have enough air to dry

and avoid rotting or developing molds. Proper air circulation is necessary because wet herbs get molds and rot.

Check every week to see how they are drying and keep checking until they are completely dry and ready to store.

Tray drying

Trays are used in many homes to dry seeds and large-leafed herbs. This is an easy way of drying herbs either indoors or outdoors. It is the best for those herbs, which have short stems that you can't tie together for hanging. Shallow-rimmed trays are most ideal and you can cover the herbs with cheesecloth.

Drying leaves

- Remove the leaves from the stems or dry them on the stems. Spread one layer of leaves evenly on the tray so they can dry fast and there can be enough air circulation.
- Place the tray with the leaves or stems in a warm, dry place that is well ventilated. Don't expose them to direct sunlight otherwise this will hasten drying.
- Turn the leaves over every day but do it gently so they don't get crushed as they dry. Drying will take about one week or so although it depends on the moisture in the plants and the temperature and humidity in that location at that time. Make sure that the herbs dry completely before you store them.
- When the leaves become crispy and they have dried completely, store them in an airtight container.

Drying seeds

- After harvesting your seeds, spread them evenly on trays in thin layers.
- Follow the same method you used to dry the leaves.

- Make sure they are completely dry and then rub them with your hands and blow off the chaff gently.
- Store the seeds in an airtight container.

There are several other methods you can use to dry herbs for use as kitchen spices and seasonings as we shall see in Chapter 4.

Items You May Need

Drying herbs on newspaper is still a method that is used by many people today. It is still viable but you should keep an eye on the herbs to avoid mildew buildup when the plants don't get enough airflow. Keep turning the herbs over so they can dry on all sides. The old method of drying plants on screens is also used to dry herbs. Old window screens come in handy especially if they are set on bricks to allow airflow from all directions. If you are using newspapers or screens keep them away from breezes to avoid wind blowing them away as they dry and become light.

Dehydrator

A dehydrating machine or dehydrator may be used to dry herbs and to speed up the drying process. This makes work easier especially if you have a bounty harvest. You can dry many herbs at the same time if you are using a dehydrator. It is also convenient and you can put herbs inside as you harvest. Herbs dried in a dehydrator usually retain their color and quality especially if dried in low temperatures. Keep checking the trays stacked inside if they have moisture and rearrange them so air can be regulated.

There are many varieties of dehydrators in the market with all the features you require. Some of them have thermostats, fans, removable and washable trays, and other features. Purchase a unit that has been approved for home use and ensure that the trays are removable and easy to clean. Choose one that fits the place that you want to keep it probably over the counter, or elsewhere.

Cheesecloth

Cheesecloth may appear to be something that is obvious in a kitchen. Although it is a simple thing, it is so handy. It really helps in the kitchen when preparing and drying herbs. Use cheesecloth to layer the plants when drying, strain herbs out of their oils, to make bouquet garni when cooking, and for other uses. The tightly woven cheesecloth types may cost more, but they are better when layering them as filters. You will need less layering of good cheesecloth while filtering. However, don't spend too much on them because you will need several of them in your kitchen.

Scales

Most of the time when you are cooking or flavoring food you put a pinch of spices and seasonings here and bits there but there are those times your recipe requires exact measurements. Invest in an Electronic kitchen scale to measure your ingredients as require. Most kitchen scales are not that expensive, but you have to look for certain basic features regardless of the price.

Features to look for:

- Most basic scales will have both American and Metric electronic measurements. This should be found in the most basic of scales.
- A Tare feature removes the weight of the container from the measurements so you can measure only the herbs added.
- The scale should be easy to clean. Glass is better as well as other non-reactive materials.

These items are in addition to other basic kitchen item, which you use to harvest, dry and store your herbs and seasonings.

Chapter 3

Tips on Harvesting Different Parts of Herbal Plants

You may grow herbs in pots or in your herb garden, at home or you may get some from a neighbor or a friend. It is important to know which parts you can harvest because you may need to do this, for one reason or another. Herbs have optimal times for harvesting them, and these times differ depending on the plant part that you need to harvest.

The following are guidelines that you should follow when harvesting each part of a herbal plant if you want to get optimal benefits for your kitchen spices and seasonings.

Leaves

Most of us use herbal leaves in the kitchen to flavor food whether it is meat, stew, soups, sauces and salads, among other foods. It is common to find fresh or dried herbs in most kitchens. Herbal leaves are used for cooking and seasoning foods. Some of them are used as preservatives and for medicinal purposes. It is important to harvest these herbs before they lose the essential oils. The best time to pick the leaves, so they can retain the essential oils is during the morning when the dew has dried. Herbal leaves picked at the right time are so nutritious and they in fact make up most of the flavoring and medicinal components.

The fresh leaves can be picked at any time of the year during the herb's growth. Most of these leaves are used immediately after harvesting, to use in recipes or in preparation of fresh tea but what do you do with the extra leaves? Dry them. When you harvest your herbal leaves from your garden for drying purposes, ensure that you collect them in the morning when the dew has dried. This should be before the sun is hot in order to preserve the essential oils. When the sun heats the plants too much, the essential oils are lost. Harvesting at the right time ensures that all or most of the essential oils are left within the leaves.

Harvest the leaves when they are still young before the plant flowers. It is best to harvest them young when the plant is in the growth stage, because this is when the leaves have most of the flavor. For evergreen herbs like Rosemary and Thyme, the leaves can be harvested just before they begin flowering to get most of their flavor.

You should also harvest as often as you can. You can even give your family and friends your dried herbs as gifts.

Whole Plants

When you want to harvest the entire herb plant or aerial parts with or without the roots, the most ideal time to harvest these parts, is just before the plant flowers. When you notice that the plant is about to flower, you can cut the whole stem or uproot the entire plant if you need the leaves. At this time, the plant will not be able to re-grow in many instances, so it will retain most of the nutrients since it would have used them for re-growth. If you plan to harvest wild herbs, and you need to dry the whole plant, you should try as much as possible to harvest less than a third of the plant.

Flowers

Flowers are usually very delicate and so you should harvest them carefully. The best time to pick flowers is at mid-day, when they are usually dry but don't harvest them when they are wet. The flowers wither easily when it is hot. They can even get spoilt as you harvest them especially in a hot day. If you put them in a container, when you are harvesting them, they will of course pile over each other and become too warm. Avoid keeping them in the container. As you pick the flowers, avoid all those that have any damages, spots or decay. Don't collect flowers that have fallen off from the plant since they should be fresh and clean for consumption. Once you have finished picking them, move them inside the house and remove them from your harvesting container or basket. Take them to the drying area as soon as possible. This will protect them from bruising. Handle flowers carefully to avoid any damage.

Seeds and Fruits

Harvesting seeds requires patience because you have to wait until they are fully grown. You have to wait until the fruits are ripe and the pods become mature before you start harvesting the seeds. The best day to harvest is when it is dry but just before the seeds get dispersed. Check to make sure the seeds are no longer green. When they turn brown or black this is when you know they are ready to be harvested. Other signals that show readiness are when the fruits have ripened enough or when the pods containing the seeds dry. Ready seeds are usually hardened and most often, they have dry pods.

Don't harvest too early and don't harvest too late. Too early means the seeds aren't ready and so they may get molds or rot as they are dried. If you harvest too late you will lose most of the seeds which will have dispersed. This means that you need to keep observing them to know the right time. The fruits that you want to dry will ripen and become red, yellow, and brown in color among other colors.

Roots

The best time to harvest herbal roots is in the fall although some gardeners also harvest them in spring. This is the time of the year when the herbal roots are full of energy. Of all herbal parts of the plant, the roots are the most powerful but you need a lot of effort to uproot some of them although not all types are difficult to harvest. Maybe this is one of the reasons why many people don't dry herbal roots and yet they are so nutritious. Many herbal roots can be uprooted with bare hands especially the small ones. Harvesting roots, which have established themselves in the soil, is hard work. Fortunately, you will get so many benefits from them as flavorings, herbal teas and infusions among other uses. Uprooting them will require some commitment on your part, but there are shortcuts you can follow to make it easier.

Important Tips:

The best way to harvest roots is to dig up the whole root system. You need to dig carefully. You can loosen the roots by using your gardening spade. Press and lift all the base of the plant and all around it, so the whole root system can come up. This is the only way you can lift free roots that spread fast and those that grow deeper into the soil. Remove the roots you want to harvest and keep them aside and then replant the rest for continued growth. Harvest only what you need by dividing the root system. Don't leave holes gaping, fill them up with soil.

Some roots harden so much when they are dried. It is therefore good to wash, peel and cut them when they are still fresh. This is the time they are soft otherwise if you dry them you will them hard to work with if you hadn't peeled and cut them into smaller pieces. Some dried roots can be so tough that it is hard to grind them in whole. They become like rocks when they're fully dried. Wash them thoroughly and scrub the dirt away if you need to. Peel and cut them as soon as you can.

Bark

Herbal bark (i.e. Cinnamon) is used to flavor foods and you can use the sticks or grind them to powder. Harvesting bark can cause the herbal tree to get damaged so you need to do it correctly so you can get hers for a long time. Don't peel the bark around the whole trunk otherwise it may not continue growing. If you do this, you will cut off the food supply that helps the tree to grow and this can make it dry and stop its growth. Harvest a little bark at a time and don't stress its growth.

Chapter 4

Methods Used for Drying Herbs

Growing and drying herbs is among the easiest forms of food preservation.

Most herbs contain little moisture and this makes it easier to preserve them almost immediately after harvesting. Drying your own herbs and spices is economical taking into consideration the high cost of spices and seasonings. When you grow your own, you know that you are getting fresh and organic spices and seasonings. You can also grow your favorite herbs and choose the varieties that you like.

Air-Drying

You can hold branches together and tie them with a string or rubber band. Smaller bundles are easier to dry and they dry much faster than large ones. Put the bundle of herbs, with the stems facing up, inside a paper bag or cover the leaves and flowers. Tie the end of the bag to close it, ensuring that you don't crush your herbs. Remember to poke a few holes in the bag so there can be air ventilation. Hang the paper bag in a warm, well-ventilated place as explained earlier. Make sure that the stems are hanged upside down so the essential oils can be retained. This way, the oils can move into the leaves. Your herbs may be dry and ready to store, within a week or so.

Drying plants in the sun or outdoors

Most people don't like this method because the plants get bleached and they lose most of the oils and flavor. Those who prefer this method use it for drying leaves and flowers for craft purposes.

Cut the plants when the dew has dried. Tie them in bundles with rubber bands. Tie the same sizes so drying can be consistent. Hang plants facing downward.

Use the porch to hang them or use a hanger and hang them where there is light. Leave them for several days to dry, but keep checking. Tie the plants securely because of the wind.

Remove them for storage when the leaves and flowers become crispy.

Drying plants indoors

To air-dry herbs indoors, you need to harvest the plants when it is dry. You can dry them as stems or flowers by tying them in bundles and hanging them upside down. This should be in a warm and dry place but you should avoid the kitchen and any sources of steam. In the kitchen there are cooking vapors, which can affect drying.

Tie the bundles using twist-ties, rubber bands or a thin-gauge wire which you can easily adjust when need arises. When the stems or flowers start drying they need the wire or thread to be tightened to hold them well since they shrink as they dry.

You can wrap the bundles with:

- Muslin
- A mesh produce bag
- A paper bag, which has several holes. The paper bag should be tied at the neck.

You may want to dry the flowers, leaves, or sprigs individually, which means that you have to lay them somewhere to dry. A drying screen, a mesh, old window screens or hardware cloths can be used. The mesh needs to be stapled or nailed to a wooden frame to avoid the drying plants from touching dirty surfaces. You can use cheesecloth to spread on the surface where you want to dry your plants, and then layer them in a single layer so they can dry well.

Drying can happen any time between hours and days. When you ensure that the herbs are completely dry, store them in dry jars and containers.

Solar Drying

Not all climates are ideal for solar drying. This requires a warm, dry weather of about 100 degrees. The humidity should be about 60 degrees or even less. When these conditions are appropriate, you can use the heat from the sun to dry your herbs naturally. However, you shouldn't expose the herbs to too much direct sunlight because they might lose essential oils and cause bleaching.

Solar drying involves:

- Placing the plants over drying screens or mesh, outside until they become brittle while transferring them indoors for the nights.
- Drying the herbs under a windshield or rear window within your car on hot days.
- Drying them in a solar food dehydrator, which you can build. You may put drying screens, which can be stacked one over the other to allow you to dry different herbs at the same time. The food dehydrator is fitted with a glass top for radiation. Install an absorbing plate to transmit the heat from the sun to the herbs. Put a vent to allow the air to circulate so the plants do not get molds.

The advantage of this method is that it is the most natural method and it is cost-efficient. You can also dry as many herbs as you want.

The disadvantage of solar drying is that not all geographical locations receive the heat of the sun that reaches 100 degrees. Some areas receive less while others receive more. Furthermore, you may want to dry your herbs and seasonings at other times not necessarily during the hot season. Humidity is also a challenge in many places.

Drying in the Refrigerator

Another simple method that you can use to dry your herbs is to put them in the fridge and leave them there. This can sound like neglect but it's not. You may have discovered that when you put the herbs in the fringe they dry on their own. This can take just a few days depending on the type of herbs. However, you should leave them without packaging otherwise they could rot. Leave the herbs open and the cold and dryness of the fridge will dry them until they become crispy. They will also retain their flavor, color, and fragrance, which make this one of the best methods to dry a few herbs.

This method was used for drying Chives and Parsley, which keep their great flavor in their dried form unlike when other methods are used. The only challenging thing you encounter while using this method is trying to find enough space in the fridge to dry all the herbs you want. If you have extra space in the fridge, dry some herbs in it especially those that lose flavor easily. Put some of your herbs in your fridge and leave them uncovered for a few days, put more as space allows. If your fridge has limited space, dry other herbs elsewhere or dry in them portions. When the first lot has dried, store them and then place more in the fridge.

Oven Drying

You may think that drying herbs and spices in the oven is easy but it may not be. You may have tried it already and if you have done so, you know that its labor intensive and it uses a lot of energy. For herbs and spices to dry thoroughly, they need to be dried at around 100 degrees, but from experience most of the ovens cannot be set that low. The herbs require air circulation, and this can become a challenge since there are ovens, which haven't been fitted with vents.

If you choose to use your oven to dry your herbs, you will need an oven thermometer to measure the heating and use it to experiment with this method. You will have to alternate between turning the oven to the lowest setting i.e. warm, and turning it off for some time. In the meantime, you should leave the oven lights on so you can watch the herbs and see if they need more heat or less.

Method:

- Herbs can be dried in an oven and will be suitable for culinary and medicinal purposes.
- Set the oven to a very low temperature, the lowest it will go. Leave the door open.
- Layer the herbs on a baking sheet and place it in the lowest level inside the oven. Alternatively, spread cheesecloth on a wire cooling rack and layer the herbs on top. This allows air circulation to take place all over. Place the rack with the spread out herbs within the oven somewhere in the middle when the temperature is around 100 degrees.
- Allow the herbs time to dry but keep turning the herbs over and over again regularly.
- Herbs dry much faster in the oven than fruits and vegetables. They dry quickly and they don't become spoilt easily. If you want to experiment with oven drying, start drying herbs before you dry fruits and vegetables. Food drying in the oven can be tricky, so you should start with herbs.
- You can open the oven slightly and check the temperature with your thermometer to ensure that, it is about 100 degrees. Lower the settings if it is more than that or switch it off for a while.

The advantage of this method is that, most people have ovens at home and so, you can dry your herbs and seasonings any day, any time.

The disadvantage is that this is the most labor-intensive method. It is also not cost-efficient because of the energy used.

Microwave Drying

You can use the microwave to dry your herbs, but this is not recommended for drying foods that have a lot of moisture. Drying herbs and seasonings using this method may not be as easy as drying them using solar-drying and electric dehydrator drying, but you can still use it for the herbs that have little moisture.

Method:

- Remove any spotted, diseased and discolored leaves. Remove the leaves from the stems and clean them. Place them between paper towels in layers.
- Cover the sheets after layering the herbs but ensure that the herbs in each towel aren't too many. Place other paper towels on top of the herbs.
- Put the herbs inside your microwave and set it on HIGH. Allow them to dry for about 2 minutes although this depends on the type of herbs you are drying.
- Check them every few seconds i.e. 30 seconds to make sure that they don't get burned.
- Set the microwave on high power for 1 minute if the herbs are brittle. Allow them to rest for 30 seconds. Alternate the drying between 30 seconds on high power and 30 seconds of resting. Most of the herbs should be dry within 10 minutes or in less time.
- Take the paper towel out of the microwave and let the herbs rest for a couple of minutes. This way the moisture from the microwave will evaporate into the air. Place the herbs on a rack or spread them on a clean cloth and let cool.

- Store your herbs in airtight jars or container. Keep the herbs away from light and heat. You can also use sealable airtight bags.

The advantage of this method is that it is easy and fast. Microwave drying also preserves the color and flavor, making it popular.

The disadvantage is that you need to be cautious otherwise you risk cooking the herbs and starting a fire if you are not careful.

Machine Dehydrating

Food dehydrators come in many sizes and the prices range from low to high. Unless you harvest a lot of plants for drying choose a medium machine that will serve the purpose. Store it in a convenient place where you can dry your spices and seasonings without struggling with the storage of the machine. Drying using this machine is easy because it has thermostats and timers. Some people even layer the plants on the tray and leave them to dry without switching on the machine.

Many of these dehydrators control the temperature and you can also adjust it when you need to. They also have a fan to circulate the air. There are round models and box-type models fitted with multiple stacking trays which are washable. You can also use them for proofing dough when baking bread and buns as well as culturing your yogurt. Always follow the manufacturer's instructions to keep your machine in good order.

CHAPTER 5

HOW YOU CAN DRY AND STORE YOUR HERBS

After harvesting, you want to dry the herbs and store them for a long time. In this chapter you will learn how you can dry and store each part of the plant, which you have harvested. You may also buy fresh herbs and dry them after using what you need. This assures you of ready supply when you want to use spices and seasonings.

Drying leaves

When you think of drying herbs and spices, the first thing you think about is drying leaves. Leaves are often the first part of a herb that most of us consider drying. Leaves are used in preparation of many herbal teas and food recipes. They are also used in many herbal crafts. You should take care of the leaves so that you retain their flavor and color as well as texture. Of course you wouldn't want crushed leaves when you need garnishing of whole leaves. Avoid development of molds and mildew on the leaves because they are not healthy. Discard such leaves and this is for your health.

To dry leaves properly you have o dry them completely. Harvest them with or without the stems, after the dew has dried, but before it becomes too hot outside. Keep these herb leaves either inside or outside, but away from direct sunlight as you pick them. This is to retain the essential oils within the plants and to avoid speeding up drying. If the herbs are clean it may not be necessary to wash them, they only need a quick shake to remove any dust and insects. That is all that you need to do, then you can start drying them. You may dry herb leaves in small bundles, while tying the stems together with a string or elastic band. You can use elastic, so that it can adjust easily as the herbs shrink to prevent them from falling. The stems will sure enough shrink as they dry because of loss of moisture.

You can also use paper bags to cover the herbal bundles. You will have to tuck the herbs in paper bags before you tie them. The paper bags protect the herbs from receiving direct sunlight and any dust particles. Furthermore, any dried leaves, which fall off from the stems, accumulate in the bag. This is best for smaller leaves such as Thyme leaves, which get caught in the paper bag instead of falling down. A dehydrating machine or dehydrator may be used to dry herbal leaves. This makes the work go a bit quicker, cutting the time it takes to dry herbs fully. Herbal leaves dried in the dehydrator in low temperatures retain their green color most of the times. Even Basil will retain its color when you dry it in low temperatures in a dehydrator with a fan, or you can flip the leaves over regularly if you don't have the fan. You can even dry leaves on newspapers or screens.

Drying Flowers

Herb flowers are very delicate, and require a gentle touch. They can be dried in the same way as herb leaves, but handled with the lightest pressure, as bruising or breaking the petals will guarantee that decay will develop.

Herbal flowers that are properly dried will retain their color and scent. If just the petal is needed, I find it easier to allow the flower head to dry for a day, and then remove the petals to finish drying. This gives the flowers a little time for the petals to loosen for easier removal.

Drying Seeds

Please, keep your herb seeds from year to year. Since most herb seeds are organic and non-GMO, you are storing the perfect specified for your growing area.

To dry herb seeds, remove the seed heads and allow them to dry in a single layer. Newspaper works well for this. Avoid anything more than the slightest breeze when drying seeds. There is nothing worse than a summer gust of wind blowing your dill seed harvest all over the barn floor. I speak from experience.

Seeds will dry very quickly, within a couple of weeks. You cannot over dry seeds in most cases, and I often dry them enough to rub the seeds from the seed head, and then jar them in mason jars with a muslin lid for another month, to allow any excess moisture that may remain, to evaporate. Then, I seal the jar and place it in a cool, dark place until needed.

Drying Roots

Herbal roots are loaded with heath benefits, which are so useful to us. Yet, they are not commonly dried like leaves and flowers are. Herbal roots are healthy and nutritious so they should be dried to make them available all the time. Although you may prefer to use fresh herbal roots it is good to dry these useful herbs.

Before you start drying, the roots should be thoroughly cleaned. Removing dirt and dust from some of the roots may become difficult due to the time they have been in the soil. You can use a vegetable scrubbing brush to scrub away all the dirt that has been trapped on the roots. Use plenty of water when cleaning and then remove the root hairs before you start the drying process. Scrub off any remaining dirt as the root dries.

There are roots that need to be peeled before they are dried and that is when they are still fresh such as Marshmallow. They have to peel first because it is hard to peel them when they are dried. There are roots such as Comfrey, which are too large for grinding especially with a home coffee grinder. You'll need to cut these roots into smaller sizes that are manageable when they are still fresh. Once the roots have been dried it becomes difficult to grind them into powder. It is even harder to grind them if the home coffee grinder has been fitted with a plastic blade.

Cut the roots and then dry them in a single layer to avoid molds. You can make your work easier by drying all your roots in a dehydrator. This ensures that your spices and seasonings lose all the moisture. You can still dry them using the other methods and they will dry effectively even on newspaper and screen, but you will have o monitor them carefully.

How to Store Dried Herbs

Storing herbs is a great way to preserve them and use them in the future. Keeping herbs in dried form is a popular way of preserving herbs and it is easy and worth doing. You can use dried herbs straight from the jars or containers when you need them. You can use them to flavor your meat, chicken, fish, stew, soup, stew and other foods when cooking or garnish your food with these spices and seasonings. You may like them in your sauces and salads. They come in many different types, colors and tastes that not only flavor the food but also make it so appetizing.

Some herbs like Mint, Thyme, Marjoram, Oregano and Rosemary dry well. You may use dried herbs just like you use fresh herbs but you need less amounts in your recipes because they are more concentrated. However, you should dry them using the right methods so you can preserve their color, flavor, fragrances or aromas. If you don't do it carefully, you may lose them in the drying process.

To know if your herbs have dried, touch them with your hands and if they crumble easily without feeling leathery, then they have dried but avoid crumbling them. It is better to dry whole leaves and whole seeds instead of in pieces because they retain most of the essential oils when they are whole. Store them as they are without crushing them and grind them when you need to use them.

Dried herbs whether they are spices or seasonings should be stored in airtight jars and containers. They should be kept away from direct light, moisture and away from heat. Avoid keeping them near your oven or pouring them into the food directly from the container when you are cooking. To make it easier for you to identify different herbs, you need to label the jars either before packing or as soon as you put the contents into them. The labels should contain the kind of content i.e. Dill. You need to indicate the date of preservation of the contents so you can know which herbs are too old. This will help you to know which ones to use first. You should specify the different varieties by writing with a felt pen or sticking labels on the jars so you can use each type for the right purpose.

The herbs and spices that have not dried completely will likely put moisture on the jars or become moldy. That is why you should check the jars a few days after packing. If you notice any droplets of moisture in the jars, you can re-dry the content and re-pack them. Any herbs or spices with molds should be thrown away and they shouldn't be used in any way.

Important Tips:

- Always store your dried herbs in airtight containers, or in plastic bags, which have zippers. This will also do. Use small canning jars, which will keep the herbs in good condition for a long time.
- Ensure that you label each jar with the name and date of the herbs in your containers.
- Transparent jars help you to choose the herbs easily if you know them but dark jars are better because they prevent them from light.
- Your herbs retain most of their flavor if you store them whole, especially the leaves and seeds. Store them whole and crush them when you want to use them.
- Any herbs that show even the slightest signs of having moulds should be discarded. Keep herb containers in an

airy, cool and dry place away from heat, moisture and direct light.
- Dried herbs are best when they are used within one year unless they are whole which can stay for many years. That is when they have optimal nutritional value. Dried herbs, which are over one year, may have lost their colour and flavour. Plan to harvest and dry herbs regularly and discard very old herbs.

Freezing Herbs

Freezing herbs is another way of preserving them. Herbs that hold a lot of moisture like many dense herbs, such as Basil, Mint, Chives, and Tarragon are best dried in a dehydrator. Another alternative is to freeze them. It's easier to freeze them than to dry them. You may prefer to freeze other herbs such as Chervil, Cilantro and Dill

Chapter 6

List of Herbs: Kitchen Spices and Seasonings

There are many spices and seasonings you can use in your kitchen. You can use the spices and seasonings the way you prefer and you should not limit yourself to what is listed while using them.

Dried Herbs and Spices

Have you ever-confused cumin with coriander or any other herbs and spices? The following are some of the herbs you can harvest, dry and store.

Asafoetida: Asafoetida or Asafetida is commonly used to aid digestion. It has a strong odor that is similar to the garlic-onion flavor. It is used in Indian cooking.

Achieve: This is a reddish-brown powder or paste, which is ground from the Annatto seeds (see below). It has an earthy flavor. Used in Mexican dishes and sauces.

Allspice: It has some similarity with Cloves and has a pungent and deep flavor. Used in spice mixes.

Annatto Seeds: These are very tough reddish-brown seeds with a woodsy aroma and an earthy flavor. They are known as Achieve powder or paste (see above) when they are ground. They are used to flavor many Mexican dishes.

Basil: This is a member of the Mint family. Basil has green leaves and a sweet Clove-like flavor and pungent. Used in the preparation of Italian and Mediterranean cuisine. Its flavor comes out best with chicken, fish, eggs, pasta, and tomatoes among other foods.

Bay Leaf: This is aromatic types of leaves from the evergreen Bay laurel tree. They are also known as laurel leaves. Bay Leaf has a woodsy, pungent flavor. Used in meats, sauces, stews, soups, vegetables and is good as background color in many foods.

Chili powder: This mixture is made up of many different herbs such as ground dried chilies, Coriander, Cumin, Garlic and Oregano, among other herbs and spices. The flavor is mild to hot. It is used in Chili, eggs and cheese, soups and stews.

Chives: These are rich in Vitamin A and belong to the onion and leek family. They have onion or garlic flavor and are used in appetizers, salads, sauces, shellfish and cream soups, among other uses.

Cilantro: These are green herbs from Coriander plants. They have a pungent, soapy fragrance. They are used in green juices and smoothies, fish, rice, salsas and salads. Cilantro is used as a flavoring and garnish. It is very popular especially in the preparation of Italian, Latin American and Mexican foods.

Cinnamon: This bark is extracted from the Cinnamon tree. It is dark reddish in color. Cinnamon sticks or ground powder can be added to food when it is cooking to add flavor. It is sweet and very aromatic. Used in the preparation of sweets, doughnuts and hot drinks. It is added to vegetables such as carrots, sweet potatoes and winter squash. Cinnamon is found in most cuisines in the world, both sweet and savory dishes.

Cloves: They have aromatic, sweet and pungent flavor. They have a strong flavor so they should be used with caution. They are reddish-brown buds from the evergreen Clove tree. Cloves are used in baking to spice cakes and cookies as well as in sauces, baked beans and as pickling. They go well with braised meat.

Coriander: This is related to the Parsley family. The seeds are obtained from the Coriander plant. The taste is a mixture of Sage,

Lemon, and Caraway flavors. It is mostly used in Mexican and Spanish recipes, sausages and pickling.

Cumin: This is hot, slightly bitter and pungent. It is common in Asian, Middle Eastern, and Mediterranean cuisine. It is used in chili and curry powder blends, lamb, fish, and pickling.

Caraway Seeds: These seeds have anise-tasting flavor and they are used in soda bread, potato salads and sauerkrauts.

Cardamom: This is a warm, aromatic spice used mostly in Indian cuisine. It is also used for baking and usually; it is combined with Cloves and Cinnamon.

Cayenne Pepper: This is obtained from dried and ground red Chili Peppers. It is used in soups; spice mixes and braises, to add a sweet, hot taste.

Chia Seeds: Although they are almost flavorless, they can be ground and added to cereals, smoothies, and baked products to make them more nutritious and add texture. They are at times used as a substitute of eggs in vegan dishes.

Coriander Seeds: These have an earthy, lemon flavor. They are used in many Mexican and Indian dishes as well as North African and Middle Eastern cuisines.

Dill Seeds: These are seeds from Dill plants. They have a tangy and pungent flavor and are used in meats, salads, sauces and vegetables.

Dill Weed: These are green leaves harvested from Dill plants. They have a tangy and pungent flavor and are used in eggs, fish, salads, sauces, vegetables, pickling and breads.

Fennel Seeds: They are greenish-brown seeds harvested from Fennel plants. They have aromatic and lightly sweet licorice flavor. They are used in breads, sausages, fish, sauces, soups and Italian dishes. These seeds are chewed on their own to freshen breath and aid digestion.

Fenugreek: It has a bitter, burnt sugar-like flavor and is used in many Indian and Middle Eastern dishes.

Garlic: This can be ground into powder made from Garlic cloves which have been dehydrated. It is used to give dishes a sweet, soft garlic flavor.

Ginger: Ginger is dehydrated and ground to give a spicy flavor. The Ginger root is slightly sweet, slightly pungent and has a spicy aroma. It is commonly used in German, Chinese, and Jamaican recipes to make Ginger tea, cookies, cakes, and marinades.

Lovage: This has a taste that is between Celery and Parsley. It is used to flavor seafood, stocks, salads and soups as well as pickling.

Marjoram: It is in the Mint and Oregano family. These oval and pale green leaves are aromatic, pungent and slightly bitter. They are used in meat, chicken, fish, sausages, and vegetables and as stuffing.

Mint: It is a very popular spice with a strong, sweet, and cool flavor. It is used to refresh beverages, and in lamb, sauces, desserts, sauces and soups.

Mustard Seeds: They are available in yellow, white, and brown colors. They have a hot, pungent flavor and are used in meats, pickling and relishes. Finely powdered mustard is used in sauces.

Nutmeg: These are oval seeds harvested from Nutmeg trees and they have a dark grey color. They are warm, nutty, and spicy and are used in the preparation of beverages, cookies, cakes, sauces and in sweet potatoes. Nutmeg has a sweet and pungent flavor. The herb does well in baked products as well as in savory dishes.

Oregano: This is a member of the Mint family. It has a strong, aromatic and pungent marjoram-like or lemony flavor because it is related to Marjoram and Thyme. Oregano is used in meat, fish, poultry, and tomatoes. It is great in Greek, Italian, Mexican dishes and Mediterranean dishes.

Paprika: This is a red pepper when powdered, which has a sweet to hot and slightly bitter flavor. It is used in stews, dips, fish, poultry, soups, and in potato and egg salads. Sprigs are used as garnish and in herb mixtures and spice blends.

Peppercorns: These are prepared from Peppercorn berries and they are available in a variety of colors. White, black, pink, and green colors are the most popular. They have a pungent, hot peppery flavor and are used to flavor meats, eggs and poultry.

Red Pepper: This is also known as Red Cayenne Pepper and its taste is hot and spicy. You should use in moderation unless you like very hot, spicy foods.

Rosemary: It has silver-green leaves and is a member of the Mint family. Rosemary has a strong and piney flavor and is great with grilled meats, fish, eggs, lamb, beans, stuffing, soups, and potatoes.

Saffron: These are yellow-orange stigmas (when dried), which are harvested from crocus plants. The herb has a pungent, aromatic flavor. It is used in stews, sauces, rice, poultry, Spanish recipes and Swedish cakes and breads. It gives foods a bright yellowish color.

Sage: This has narrow, oval leaves, which have gray-greenish color. It has a slightly bitter taste and is used in pork, chicken, sausages, duck, goose and stuffing. Sage has a pine-like flavor, which is lemony and eucalyptus-like.

Sesame Seeds: These are tiny, flat seeds, which are brown, red or black in color. They have a nutty and slightly sweet taste and texture. These seeds are used in breads, cookies, cakes, salad dressings and seafood.

Terragon: It has narrow, pointed leaves, which are dark in color. This herb has a slightly licorice flavor and is used in meats, eggs, poultry, pickling, salads, and sauces.

Thyme: This is a member of the Mint family, which has gray-green leaves. It has pungent, woodsy tea-like flavor and is used in meats, fish, poultry, soups, vegetables and potatoes. Thyme is an all-purpose seasoning.

Turmeric: This is a yellow-orange root, which can be ground into powder when dry. It is related to Ginger and is used to add color to food. It has a pungent, mildly woodsy, earthy and slightly bitter taste and is used in curries, American mustard and East Indian cuisine. Turmeric is at times used because of the yellow color than because of its flavor.

Some Fresh Herbs

You may use the following herbs either as fresh, frozen or dried spices and seasoning.

Basil: This has aromatic flavor and is used in pasta dishes, or in sandwich stuffing.

Chervil: This has a delicate anise flavor and is used in salads and as garnish.

Chives: These have onion flavor and they are used as garnish.

Cilantro: This is harvested from Coriander plants. Cilantro leaves and stems have a pungent flavor and is used in Latin American, Caribbean, and Asian cooking.

Dill: This is a light feathery herb with a pungent flavor. It is use for pickling, and with fish, and potatoes among other uses.

Fenugreek: This smells like maple syrup when it is cooking, but it has a flavor that is bitter, burnt and sugar-like.

Marjoram: This has a floral and woodsy flavor and is used in sauces and marinades.

Mint: This has an intense flavor and is used in chocolate, chewing gum and with lamb, peas, and potatoes.

Oregano: It has a lemony flavor and it is commonly used in Mexican and Mediterranean dishes.

Parsley: This is a very popular herb, which is ether flat or curly, and it has a light and grassy flavor.

Rosemary: This has a strong and piney flavor and is good in eggs, grilled meat, beans, and potatoes.

Sage: it has a pine-like flavor, which is more like lemon and eucalyptus.

Conclusion

There are so many other herbs than you can find. However, what you needed to know is how to harvest, clean, dry and store your kitchen spices and seasonings. Whatever plants you want to dry, you can use the methods explained in this book. You will enjoy herbs that you have dried yourself than those you buy. This is because you know what you have stored is fresh, organic and long lasting.

Drying herbs is interesting and it can be fun. You can ask your kids or hubby to help in harvesting, drying and storing them. They will find it fun. Share these moments to connect with each other as you work. You will enjoy the time you spend together drying herbs that flavor your food. You can ask them to choose their particular varieties. Some will choose the spices and seasoning based on flavor, smell and color while other will prefer to dry the easier ones.

Create time and start drying your herbs and you will have fun as you become healthier. Start with the leaves because they are easier to dry. Follow what is recommended in this book and you will be glad that you did.

ALL RIGHTS RESERVED. No part of this publication may be reproduced or transmitted in any form whatsoever, electronic, or mechanical, including photocopying, recording, or by any informational storage or retrieval system without express written, dated and signed permission from the author.

Printed in Great Britain
by Amazon